Pee-Yo-Pants Joke Book for Kids:
Over 140 Hilarious Knock-Knock Jokes, Riddles, and Tongue Twisters

(Perfect Stocking Stuffers Gift)

By: Julie Cohen

Table of Contents

Knock Knock Jokes

Knock, knock.
  Who's there?
Robin.
  Robin who?
Robin you! Give me all your money!

Knock, knock.
  Who's there?
Mercy.
  Mercy who?
Mercy beaucoup for coming today!

Knock, knock.
　　Who's there?
Taylor
　　Taylor who?
Taylor my pants, please. They're ripped!

Knock, knock.
　　Who's there?
Eunice.
　　Eunice who?
Eunice to everyone and everyone be nice to you.

Knock, knock.
　　Who's there?
Swing low.
　　Swing low who?
Sweet low, sweet chariot.

Knock, knock.
　　Who's there?
Tween.
　　Tween who?
Tween this and that.

Knock, knock.
   Who's there?
Hugh.
   Hugh who?
Hugh who, I just got an 'A' on my test!

Knock, knock.
   Who's there?
Tattoo.
   Tattoo who?
Not me! My parents would kill me if I got a tattoo!

Knock, knock.
   Who's there?
You.
   You who?
You who is my favorite chocolate drink.

Knock, knock.
   Who's there?
Ya.
   Ya who?
Ya who isn't the search engine I use. Try again.

Knock, knock.
Who's there?
Russian.
Russian who?
Russian you to finish this joke!

Knock, knock.
Who's there?
Icicle.
Icicle who?
Icicle of these awful jokes!

Knock, knock.
Who's there?
Rock.
Rock who?
Rock beats scissors!

Knock, knock.
Who's there?
Yule.
Yule who?
Yule love how I decorated my room for Christmas!

Knock, knock.
Who's there?
Nat King Cole.
Nat King Cole who?
Nat King Cole, so give him some hot chocolate to warm up!

Knock, knock.
Who's there?
Honey bee.
Honey bee who?
Honey bee a dear and get my tea!

Knock, knock.
Who's there?
Cyber Ian.
Cyber Ian who?
Cyber Ian Huskies are my favorite type of dog!

Knock, knock.
Who's there?
Weave.
Weave who?
Weave got to buy this basket!

Knock, knock.
    Who's there?
Fisher.
    Fisher who?
Fisher meat for dinner?

Knock, knock.
    Who's there?
Otto.
    Otto who?
Otto correct keeps changing my texts!

Knock, knock.
    Who's there?
Knot.
    Knot who?
Knot going to keep asking me "Knock, knock. Who's there?" are you?

Knock, knock.
    Who's there?
Butter.
    Butter who?
Butter stop asking me "Who's there!"

Knock, knock.
Who's there?
Thyme.
Thyme who?
Thyme to add the rosemary to the chicken!

Knock, knock.
Who's there?
Missouri.
Missouri who?
Missouri loves company!

Knock, knock.
Who's there?
Ivan two.
Ivan two who?
Ivan two drink your blood!

Knock, knock.
Who's there?
Pool.
Pool who?
Pool up your swimsuit!

Knock, knock.
Who's there?
Hope.
Hope who?
Hope you want to hear another knock knock joke!

Knock, knock.
Who's there?
Beaver.
Beaver who?
Beaver you do another knock knock joke, warn me!

Knock, knock.
Who's there?
Holland.
Holland who?
Holland Oates are my parents' favorite musicians!

Knock, knock.
Who's there?
Oil can.
Oil can who?
Oil can stain your shirt!

Knock, knock.
Who's there?
Harry.
Harry who?
Harry people are warmer than non-hairy people!

Knock, knock.
Who's there?
Witch doctor.
Witch doctor who?
Witch doctor do you need to see, heart or eye doctor?

Knock, knock.
Who's there?
Monk E.C.
Monk E.C. who?
Monk E.C. monkey do!

Knock, knock.
Who's there?
Harold.
Harold who?
Harold dog is thirty-two!

Knock, knock.
Who's there?
Hail.
Hail who?
Hail to the Chief is the Presidential anthem!

Knock, knock.
Who's there?
Idaho.
Idaho who?
Idaho the dirt before planting those potatoes if I were you!

Knock, knock.
Who's there?
Mitch Egan.
Mitch Egan who?
Mitch Egan state is where you'll find Detroit and Grand Rapids!

Knock, knock.
Who's there?
Wine.
Wine who?
Wine all you want, I'm not giving in!

Knock, knock.
Who's there?
Runoff.
Runoff who?
Runoff and find your brother!

Knock, knock.
Who's there?
Noah.
Noah who?
Noah better joke than this one?

Knock, knock.
Who's there?
Dogwood.
Dogwood who?
Dogwood eat my dinner if I let him!

Knock, knock.
Who's there?
Hail.
Hail who?
Hail a cab when you need a ride!

Knock, knock.
   Who's there?
Ant.
   Ant who?
Ant you gonna ask me who's coming to the picnic?

Knock, knock.
   Who's there?
Alpaca.
   Alpaca who?
Alpaca lunch to take with us!

Knock, knock.
   Who's there?
Egg.
   Egg who?
Egg cellent weather we've been having!

Knock, knock.
   Who's there?
Board.
   Board who?
Board already? Then read more knock knock jokes!

Knock, knock.
Who's there?
Charger.
Charger who?
Charger cash for that phone you're buying?

Knock, knock.
Who's there?
Modem.
Modem who?
Modem weeds taking over the grass or there's no dessert for you!

Knock, knock.
Who's there?
Italic.
Italic who?
Italic like I see it!

Knock, knock.
Who's there?
Icon.
Icon who?
Icon not tolerate anymore computer knock knock jokes!

Knock, knock.
　Who's there?
Catcher.
　　Catcher who?
Catcher before she falls!

Knock, knock.
　Who's there?
Locker.
　　Locker who?
Locker up before she escapes!

Knock, knock.
　Who's there?
Sticker.
　　Sticker who?
Sticker in the back room so she can nap!

Knock, knock.
　Who's there?
Letter.
　　Letter who?
Letter have a cookie so she'll stop crying!

Knock, knock.
    Who's there?
Wood.
    Wood who?
Wood you like to know what's for dinner?

Knock, knock.
    Who's there?
Locks.
    Locks who?
Locks and cream cheese taste great on a bagel!

Knock, knock.
    Who's there?
Cat gut.
    Cat gut who?
Cat gut your tongue? You're very quiet today!

Knock, knock.
    Who's there?
Poker.
    Poker who?
Poker like that, and she'll get mad at you!

Knock, knock.
Who's there?
Trailer.
Trailer who?
Trailer through the woods until you find her!

Knock, knock.
Who's there?
Meteor.
Meteor who?
Meteor steaks can't be found at any other restaurant!

Knock, knock.
Who's there?
Meter.
Meter who?
Meter down by the lake for a picnic!

Knock, knock.
Who's there?
Icing.
Icing who?
Icing my favorite songs in the shower!

Knock, knock.
Who's there?
Sweeper.
Sweeper who?
Sweeper off her feet when you dance tonight!

Knock, knock.
Who's there?
Olive.
Olive who?
Olive how you've decorated your house!

Knock, knock.
Who's there?
Candy.
Candy who?
Candy come out and play?

Knock, knock.
Who's there?
Tulips.
Tulips who?
Tulips are better than one for kissing!

Knock, knock.
Who's there?
Hell.
Hell who?
Hell leave without paying the bill!

Knock, knock.
Who's there?
Singer.
Singer who?
Singer a lullaby to put her to sleep!

Knock, knock.
Who's there?
Isle.
Isle who?
Isle be glad to get off this island!

Knock, knock.
Who's there?
Holly Daize.
Holly Daize who?
Holly Daize are my favorite time of year!

Knock, knock.
Who's there?
China.
China who?
China light over there so I can see better!

Knock, knock.
Who's there?
Iran.
Iran who?
Iran away when I realized I wasn't wearing pants!

Knock, knock.
Who's there?
Ima.
Ima who?
Ima glad this is the last knock knock joke!

What Am I? Riddles

Despite my name,
I'm not very fast.
One step in me,
Might be your last!
What am I?
   A: Quick Sand

My bed is full of rocks
And may be wet,
Not to mention full of fish!
What am I?
   A: River

For crossing rivers,
I can't be beat.
Above the earth,
People pound me,
With their feet.
What am I?
    A: Bridge

I can be mistaken for an ocean,
Though I contain no water.
I often follow the letter B,
But compared to me,
F is hotter.
What am I?
    A: Letter "C"

Attached to me you will find
A basket with a hole.
Sink a ball through me,
Then watch it bounce or roll.
What am I?
    A: Basketball hoop

I never get dizzy,
Even when I spin.
I'll find any direction,
From the city I'm in.
What am I?
> A: Compass

I go up and down,
But never around.
Moving one way at a time,
Saving you the long, hard climb.
What am I?
> A: Escalator

I'm great with hair,
But have none of my own.
While I do have teeth,
I can't eat a scone!
What am I?
> A: Comb

Liquid goes through me.
Horses chomp on me.
People ride me.
And scarecrows use me.
What am I?
> A: Straw

I may have a tail or two,
Or maybe none at all,
When I plan on going to,
A fancy social ball.
What am I?
    A: Girl with a ponytail(s)

I'm not related to the cute and furry rabbit,
Even though you chase me from household habit.
Using air currents as my guide,
Under beds and dressers I shall hide.
What am I?
    A: Dust Bunny

I destroy things around me,
Making everything wet and grey.
But when you look me in my eye,
I'm calmer, night or day.
What am I?
    A: Tropical storm

Avoiding me could cost you hours or days
As I cut through whole mountains,
Hiding from rain, sun, and haze.
What am I?
    A: Tunnel

While I look like a ribbon,
I am bigger than a tent.
Colorful as I am,
For wrapping, I'm not meant.
What am I?
  A: Rainbow

I have a nose and two wings
And more than one back seat.
Go ahead, dive from me,
And land on both your feet.
What am I?
  A: Airplane

I can be a stone
Or I can be a bean.
But I sound like I connect
A child's lower and upper leg.
What am I?
  A: Kidney

A hard horse that kids ride
With music as my guide.
Only in circles do I glide,
With bright colors I am dyed.
What am I?
  A: Merry-go-round

You might go ape over me,
As I delight your tongue.
With three scoops and a cherry,
I'm liked by old and young.
What am I?
    A: Banana sundae

I'm skinny and pointy
And hold things in place.
Hit me on my head,
And I won't give chase.
What am I?
    A: Nail

I have 4 or 5 sets of eyes,
But cannot see.
I have a tongue,
But cannot speak to thee.
What am I?
    A: Sneaker

I use numbers
To guard your treasure.
Your mind holds the key
To this security measure.
What am I?
    A: Combination lock

Short Riddles

Q: Why do cows often moo when farmers milk them?
A: Because the farmers' hands are utterly freezing!

Q: Why did the dog punch the punching bag?
A: He was a boxer!

Q: Why did the bear go to the riverbank?
A: Could you imagine what would happen if a bear used a bank in the middle of town?

Q: Why do jewelers love to vacation on Saturn?
A: To see its rings!

Q: What do asteroids use to stay together?
A: A belt.

Q: Which state has the greatest number of jokes?
A: Punnsylvania!

Q: Why did the fastest cat in class get kicked out of school?
A: He was a cheetah!

Q: Why did the corn stalk ask the farmer to repeat everything he said?
A: The corn stalk had only one ear.

Q: What did the seedling call its father?
A: Poppyseed!

Q: What did the woman say to the chef who used over 20 herbs in the soup?
A: It was dill-icious!

Q: **Name a bone that is found outside the body of certain musicians?**
A: Trombone!

Q: **Why did the house moan and groan after having new windows installed?**
A: The windowpane was too much to bear!

Q: **Why did the train crack up pulling into the station?**
A: It was loco!

Q: **What did the geometry teacher drive to school every day?**
A: A boxcar!

Q: **Why was the musician kicked out of the fish cannery?**
A: He tried to tune-a-fish!

Q: **How did the pumpkin feel when no one picked him for the team?**
A: Squashed!

Q: What baseball food is good to eat on October 31?
A: Halloweenies!

Q: How did the pump and nap know each other?
A: They're all kin!

Q: Why did the vampire return his steak?
A: It gave him chest pains.

Q: What does a mule use to get into the barn?
A: A donkey.

Q: Why did the surfer swim back to shore?
A: He couldn't wave good-bye.

Q: Linda's phone couldn't locate her mother. Why?
A: It wasn't a smart phone.

Q: Why did Moses smash the tablets on Mt. Sinai?
A: There was no wifi thousands of years ago.

Q: Why did the beans jump into the pot?
A: They were chili!

Q: Why did Dr. Frankenstein sew his monster's head closed at the laundromat?
A: To keep him from getting brainwashed.

Q: What is the worst type of cup to pour hot tea into?
A: A buttercup!

Q: When Dave drove to work, it never cost him money. Why?
A: He used the freeway.

Q: Why did Charlie keep running off with the soccer ball?
A: He's the goalkeeper!

Q: Why didn't Cinderella want to admit the glass slipper was hers?
A: She'd get in trouble for wearing her slippers out of the house!

Q: What happens when you use spot remover on a leopard?
A: Nothing. A leopard can't change its spots and neither can you!

Q: What do you call someone who throws all the hedges into her cart at the garden center?
A: Hedgehog!

Q: What can you say about Paul and Pat when they squeezed into the tiny space craft?
A: They were like two Ps in a pod!

Q: Where is the best place to sit when a submarine is diving?
A: Inside!

Q: Why did the lawyer show up in court in his underwear?
A: He forgot his lawsuit.

Q: Name a type of jelly that tastes so woody it stops traffic.
A: Logjam.

Q: What is the nun's favorite toy to play with?
A: Praydough!

Q: Why didn't the hammerhead shark feel well?
A: His head was pounding.

Q: Why did the yeast stop telling jokes to the bread?
A: He couldn't get a rise out of her.

Q: Which day of the week does 3 follow?
A: Twosday.

Q: What's the difference between a human and a mink?
A: You'll never see a mink wearing a human coat.

Q: For which crimes are cats most known?
A: Kitty littering.

Q: Why can you have tea for two or even three, but not four?
A: Four starts with the letter "F".

Q: Why do actions speak louder than words?
A: Words can't speak!

Q: Why did the judge demand the basketball player wait for him to speak?
A: The ball was in his court.

Q: What should you do if you bite off more than you can chew?
A: Spit it out!

Q: Why are geologists trying to mine clouds?
A: Every cloud has a silver lining!

Q: Why was Alexander Graham's invention of the telephone a waste of time?
A: He could have heard everything through the grapevine!

Q: Why is it a good idea to let sleeping dogs lie?
A: Because they get grumpy when you wake them!

Q: What's the best thing you can do for someone who's not playing with a full deck?
A: Buy him a new deck!

Q: What type of insect is commonly found in libraries?
A: Bookworms!

Q: Which is the happiest capital in the U.S.?
A: Annapolis, the capital of MERRY-LAND!

Q: Which U.S. state begins with the letter Y?
A: Y-O-Ming!

Q: If Godzilla looked more like a fish than a dinosaur, what would we call it?
A: Codzilla!

Q: How do you know when a snake is upset?
A: It gets hiss-terical!

Q: What are the most popular computers in Scotland?
A: MacIntosh!

Q: Why was the teenager no longer allowed online without a license?
A: He crashed the computer!

Q: Why did the knight use poison instead of his sword to kill the mythical winged fire-breathing creature?
A: He didn't want the fight to drag-on.

Q: Why isn't "Werewolf" spelled with an 'H'?
A: No one wants to scream "Herewolf"!

Q: What does a corn spider spin?
A: Cobwebs!

Q: What does a cat in pain say?
A: Me-ow!

Q: What is a tree's favorite drink?
A: Root beer.

Q: The Bearded Lady from the circus went to the pet store to buy a pet. What did she buy?
A: A bearded dragon.

Q: **When the camel asked for sugar with his tea, what did the waitress ask?**
A: "One hump or two?"

Q: **Which animal loves the Pansy flower?**
A: Chimpanzee!

Q: **What type of bees do dogs love to catch?**
A: Frisbees!

Q: **What is a volcano's favorite dessert?**
A: Lava cake!

Q: **How do you know when two spiders get married?**
A: They tie the knot!

Q: **How did the mother plant know her son would love gymnastics?**
A: He was a tumble weed!

Q: In the Eastern U.S., chefs use a blender to make milkshakes. What do chefs use out West?
A: Earthquakes!

Q: What did the hose call the water gun?
A: Little squirt.

Q: How do you get into your house on Thanksgiving?
A: With a turkey!

Q: How do people from Paris greet one another?
A: With a French kiss!

Q: What do crocodiles cook with?
A: Crockpots!

Q: What do people in France like to eat with eggs?
A: French toast!

Q: What do people from Holland like to eat on asparagus?
A: Hollandaise sauce!

Q: What do you call it when somebody stumbles and falls on a grassy area?
A: A field trip!

Q: What do dust bunnies use to cook their meals?
A: Dustpans!

Q: How do you know the teeth were excited when they got braces?
A: They were wired!

Q: It was very hot outside. What did Brenda say when Martin fixed the air conditioner?
A: "Fan-tastic!"

Q: Where do vampires invest their money?
A: Blood banks!

Q: What did the cavemen say when they cooked their meat for the first time on July 4th?
A: "Fire works!"

Q: What type of musical group likes to wrap itself around its music?
A: A rubber band!

Q: What is a zombie's favorite food?
A: Ghoulash soup!

Q: What is a cow's favorite type of snow?
A: Cornflakes!

Q: What do shoe cobblers like to eat?
A: Shoefly pie!

Q: What's a ball that you don't throw, shoot, eat, spit, bounce, or catch?
A: Eyeball!

Q: Where do roses sleep at night?
A: In their flowerbed!

Q: What do British zombies eat for dessert?
A: Kidney pie!

Q: Why do zombies love to eat sneakers?
A: Each one has a tongue!

Q: What did the mother say to her son when she caught him playing with his alphabet soup?
A: "Mind your Ps and Qs!"

Q: Why did the vampire suddenly stop at the intersection?
A: He was at a crossroads.

Q: Why did the scissors kick the joke out of the book?
A: It didn't make the cut.

Q: What is a common kitchen danger in Athens?
A: Greece fire.

Q: What do turtles, eggs, and beaches all have?
A: Shells

Long Riddles

Q: Mary's glass of milk is half full. What happened to the other half of the glass?

A: The other half of the glass is still there. It's the milk that's missing!

Q: You can visit Adam, but if you step on his property, you could kill him! Adam works hard making tunnels on tables and in bedrooms. Where does he live?

A: On an ant farm!

Q: Bob bought a junkyard, certain it would be a great place for his dog Jackson to run around and play. Jackson sniffed here and there, then plopped himself down in the middle of all the trash and barked. Bob figured out that Jackson was depressed. How?

A: The dog was down in the dumps!

Q: I can defeat my opponent by using my fists, but without ever touching him. How?

A: By winning at the game "Rock Paper Scissors."

Q: A boy found an old brass lamp and promptly rubbed the side. Out came the genie, announcing the boy could have one wish. The boy wished for a million bucks. When the boy's mother came home, she screamed. Why?

A: The genie tricked him by filling the house with a million male deer, not a million dollars.

Q: A train derailed off its tracks and plunged into the ravine below. The train was crushed beyond repair, but no one was hurt, including the engineer. Why?

A: It was a model train.

Q: A family was driving on an isolated road in Norway when they came to a bridge. This bridge was the only way to cross over the gorge. A hairy beast standing inside a kiosk blocked the bridge. He grunted and showed his sharp teeth. The family knew exactly what to do. They threw coins at the beast and immediately both the beast and the kiosk disappeared, allowing them to cross the bridge. Why?

A: It was a Troll Booth!

Q: The case of the missing oysters had gone unsolved for weeks, but finally the police cracked the case. Unfortunately, the judge had to release the thief when the star witness Mr. Clam got up to testify. Why?

A: He clammed up!

Q: A boy complained to his mother that his sister was beating him with a stick. The boy had no injuries and the stick could not be found anywhere. What happened to the stick?

A: The girl ate it (it was a breadstick).

Q: The legendary Big Foot doesn't run, but hops through the forest. How do we know this?

A: He only has one foot, or he'd be known as Big Feet. And with only one foot, hopping is more likely than running!

Q: If the Rams were to compete against the Dolphins in the Super Bowl, who would win?

A: The Rams. Dolphins couldn't stay out of water long enough to eat a whole bowl of food, let alone a Super Bowl!

Q: What happened when a bee landed on Rudolph the Red-Nosed Reindeer's nose?

A: He became known as Rudolph the Bread-nosed Reindeer.

Q: Construction came to a halt when the workers could not reach the top floor of the new building. They needed a crane to hoist the twenty-foot-long beam to the top floor. When the crane arrived, the workers realized it would never be able to lift the beam, even though the beam was made out of a lightweight material. What went wrong?

A: The crane that arrived was a bird!

Q: Why did the grandmother think her grandson had roses growing out of the sides of his head?

A: He told her he had ear buds!

Q: John and Gina were at a baseball game when he proposed to her. He said he bought a diamond for her, but it wouldn't fit on her finger. When she asked him where the diamond was so she could see it, he told her to look at the infield. Gina still didn't see the diamond. Why not?

A: She was looking for a diamond that's a jewel and didn't realize it was the baseball diamond that John was talking about.

Q: The teacher knew someone had been posting the answers to the homework online. She suspected Rose, Gerry, and Beth, but wasn't sure which one was guilty. When she walked around the room, the answer became obvious. Beth's computer had glue on it, Gerry's computer had chalk, and Rose's had marker all over it. Who was guilty?

A: Beth. She had spent the morning copying and pasting online!

Q: The triangle said to the circle, "You go around and around with no beginning or end." What did the circle reply?
A: "You have a point."

Q: The police officer had three trees in custody: a Maple, a Willow, and a Fir. He was sure one of the trees had rooted through the underground pipes. After one look at his suspects, he knew the Willow was guilty. How did he know this?
A: It was a weeping Willow.

Q: In most of the U.S., clocks spring forward in March, which is known as Daylight Savings Time. In November, they fall back. Hawaii doesn't use Daylight Savings Time. How does this prove it's better to live in Hawaii?
A: In Hawaii, the clocks are easier to hold onto because they're not jumping all over the place!

Q: Why were the railroad track's left and right rails upset with their working conditions?
A: Despite working next to each other for years, the two rails would never meet.

Q: When the Golden Goose laid its first egg for Jack's mom, she yelled something to Jack. Jack ran in, scooped up the goose, and climbed back up the beanstalk. He left the goose for the Giant with a note attached that read, "Dear Giant, your goose lays vegetables, not gold. We don't need any more vegetables so you can have the goose back." What did Jack's mom shout that made him think the egg laid vegetables?

A: "This egg is 14 karats!"

Q: The bicycle and unicycle married and had a son. Their son was going onto the bike path alone for the very first time. What did his mom shout to cheer him on?

A: "Try-cycle!"

Q: A young sassy maple tree wore a bright purple tie, causing all the other trees in the forest to moan and groan because of the horrible color. Tired of the other trees complaining, the tree said, "I'll wear any tie I want." What did the other trees reply?

A: "Not in our neck of the woods!"

Q: Sir Percy removed his armor and entered the castle to ask the princess for her hand in marriage. Before he entered, he knew that he would listen to whatever she said. When Sir Percy reached the main hall, the princess was singing a Christmas song. Sir Percy turned around and left without ever saying a word. Why?

A: She was singing Silent Knight!

Q: A magic spell made all the school supplies in a 5th grader's desk come alive. The stapler was chasing everyone, and the markers were writing all over the books. Everything was fighting. They needed someone to lead them. Whom did they choose?

A: The ruler!

Q: The art project was almost complete, but the bottle of glue only had a few drops of glue left. What did the tape dispenser say to the glue to keep him from panicking?

A: "Keep it together!"

Q: Who won the race between a sausage and two eggs?

A: The eggs. They scrambled to the finish.

Q: Why did the center bowling pin say to the two end pins that were wobbling back and forth?

A: "Straighten up before you end up in the gutter!"

Q: There were 5 dogs in the yard when a stray cat entered. The cat ran up a maple tree for safety. Only one dog followed. What happened to the other 4 dogs?

A: They ran to the oak. They were definitely barking up the wrong tree!

Q: The tennis racket was concerned that the tennis ball would never be the same after surgery. What did the tennis ball have to say about that?

A: "Don't worry, I'll bounce back!"

Q: What did the mom say when she found out her son had been shuffling his feet on the carpet and zapping everyone with a static electric charge?

A: "His behavior is shocking!"

Q: In the small town of Mystery, Bermuda, Eric kept losing his instrument before concert practice. Which instrument did he play?

A: The Bermuda Triangle!

Q: The toilet paper was getting close to the end of its life. The nearby towel shouted, "Get out of there, before it's all over for you!" What did the toilet paper reply?

A: "I can't quit yet. I'm on a roll!"

Q: The pumpkins were still sitting on their vines in the field, waiting to be picked. They were talking about Halloween. When Jack O'Lantern approached, what did they ask him?

A: "What's the scoop, Jack?"

Q: Olivia took a trip to Australia. She had a great time seeing the kangaroos and koalas, but she had trouble finding the bathroom. Why?

A: She forgot it was Outback!

Q: How do you know when a zombie was the last to use a deck of cards?

A: All the hearts have been eaten!

Q: Jessica hid the peanut butter on the roof where she knew her brother Max would never find it. Max asked Jessica when their mother would be home. Jessica answered, "1pm." Based on her answer, Max figured out where the peanut butter was without ever having to climb onto the top of the house. How did he figure it out?

A: The moment Jessica opened her mouth to speak, Max could see the peanut butter was stuck to the roof of her mouth!

Q: When asked how much 3 + 6 was, the man said "9." Then he said he was Wrong. Was he right or wrong?

A: Both. He was right about the answer to the math problem, but his name was "Wrong!"

Q: The vampire refused to ride trains. Why?

A: The crossings were killing him!

Q: If amusement park candy had a choice, from what material would their wrappers be made?

A: Cotton, of course. Whoever heard of eating polyester candy?

Q: Matt went over to Dee's house to watch an opera on TV. He asked her why she told him to bring soap. What did she reply?

A: "Because we're watching a Soap Opera!"

Q: What did the bridge say to the ship as the engineer raised both sides?

A: "It's a draw!"

Q: Why did Peter Pan fly to his island and leave without landing?

A: Someone had put up a sign: "Never Land".

Q: Where does the King of Diamonds hang out when no one is using the deck of cards?

A: It's hard to say for sure, as there are many clubs in the deck!

Q: A man was upset because his favorite shirt had a lot of wrinkles, and he needed it for work that day. He took the shirt to the dry cleaners. What did the woman who worked there say?

A: "Don't worry, we'll iron things out."

Q: What occurs naturally, is out of this world, and could be mistaken for jewelry if your finger were 175,000 miles wide?

A: Saturn's rings.

Tongue Twisters

Rain ruined Walley's white wool wrap.

Gwyn grows great grapes.

Bagel, Bible, bingo.

Willy Rabbit races Wacky Ricky.

Sioux City Sally ships shoes south.

Judge George jumps jeeps.

Bongo, bugle, beagle.

Sheriff Sharon sells six sushi.

Sally saves six sick sheep.

Nelson knows no nose news.

Peter plants purple peppers.

Fred from France found four furry ferrets.

Tracy took travel tinker toys.

Sean's silk shirt seamed short.

Shannon shepherds sheep to the shearing chute.

Ned dined near bear dens.

Don't drop chopsticks.

Kissing cousin Carol cancelled the Christmas concert.

Wee Willy Wally walked well with waffles.

Pick a purple pillow.

Made in the USA
San Bernardino, CA
01 December 2017